An Angel,
a Miracle,
OR simply
God at Work?

An Angel, a Miracle, OR simply God at Work?

By David J. Smith

CLC ✦ PUBLICATIONS
Fort Washington, Pennsylvania 19034

Published by CLC ✦ Publications

U.S.A.
P.O. Box 1449, Fort Washington, PA 19034

GREAT BRITAIN
51 The Dean, Alresford, Hants. SO24 9BJ

AUSTRALIA
P.O. Box 419M, Manunda, QLD 4879

NEW ZEALAND
10 MacArthur Street, Feilding

ISBN 0-87508-636-5

DEDICATION

To Linda, my loving wife and
second-best gift from God.

To Andrew, our second-born who
finally gets to be first.

To Becky, our first-born who is
out of the nest and flying well.

Linda and David Smith

Contents

Introduction

"If I could see just one real miracle, I know I'd never doubt again."

Have you heard someone say those words or something similar? Have you said it yourself? Have you perhaps seen a real miracle? Did it help? Did you quit doubting?

I don't know if *I* have ever seen a miracle. After you read some of the accounts in this book, however, you may want to disagree with me. Instantaneous healing, gasoline that doesn't burn, cooking gas that doesn't run out—aren't these miracles? I set extremely high standards for a verifiable miracle. Oh yes, I *believe* in miracles. I'm just not sure I have *seen* one, which is the reason for writing this book.

Do you have to see a miracle in order to see *God at work*? What about the cumulative evidence of dozens, or hundreds, or even thousands of little things that God does over a period of years or a lifetime? This is probably the norm for most Christians I know. They have not seen the "dramatic"—such as the blind man enabled to see, or the cripple suddenly leaping, or the storm stilled or the dead raised. They have seen God obviously at work in "smaller" ways, if smaller is the appropriate word. Their faith has increased over the years, not due to dramatic miracles but due to God's personal involvement in their lives and the lives of those they know. This is how I believe *my* faith has grown.

In picking experiences to share I chose several of the most dramatic and memorable— some that are closest to miraculous from my perspective. I also chose some that may seem almost mundane. These are also encouragers and faith builders, and hopefully you will then see many comparable experiences in your life.

Were some of these angelic interventions? Were some miracles? Or were they all simply God at work in the life of one of His children? I'll leave it for you to decide. My goal is to encourage you to look at your own life and to allow this to strengthen your faith as you consider how God is working for and in *you*, and hopefully *through you*. Don't make comparisons. God called Linda and me into some unusual situations and did many things appropriate for the situations. His workings in your life will be appropriate for His calling for *you*.

Chapter 1

Brought to Christ

I have been a speaker for many years. Audiences, I find, identify more with me and my message if they have some background testimony. It adds credibility to what I have to say. I assume the same is true for you, my readers. This chapter covers the first twenty years of my life.

I was born into a military family. My father was a professing non-Christian and my mother a professing Christian. But while there was no question of her religiosity, it is doubtful that she had a personal relationship with Jesus. However, she felt church to be essential, so she and I, and my younger sister, Bobbie, attended regularly. We attended services at a number of military chapels and traditional churches in the various places we lived. My recollection of church and religious teaching prior to the sixth grade is almost nonexistent, but I suspect that the churches we attended in Washington and Alaska in those years were not evangelical. I do know the ones in North

Carolina and Colorado, when I was in grades six through twelve, were not.

I may have had some godly, evangelical Sunday school teachers. I remember almost nothing about Sunday school, however, except that it was generally pleasant. Youth group on Sunday evenings was social and interactive, but not biblically oriented. While I learned very little about Jesus and the gospel, I enjoyed both Sunday school and youth group, so I had positive feelings about church in general.

My basic theology which I learned or developed in church can be summarized in five points: (1) Theistic evolution is the most plausible explanation for the existence of the universe; and if not that, then pure evolution is the answer. (2) There may or may not be a literal heaven, but there certainly is no literal hell. (3) All major religions are probably equally valid. (4) Religions exist to give moral guidelines, and when mankind finally evolves morally as far as he has scientifically, he won't need religion. (5) The Bible is not the Word of God, but it does contain the word of God—as does any book, picture, musical composition, or anything else that helps someone lead a better life.

My father was transferred to Izmir, Turkey, in the fall of 1966 after I graduated from high school in Denver. I chose to accompany my family to Turkey rather than begin college in the States. The next three months were wonderful: I loved Turkey.

We lived in civilian housing in the city of Izmir rather than on the military base. Since I was not going to school, I spent hours each day on the streets of Izmir. I began learning the language, meeting the people, eating the food and making friends.

Islam impressed me. One of my friends, Halil, planned to become a mullah one day. His commitment and that of many others to the tenets of Islam was very visible. At prayer time five times each day they would stop and pray, whether they were at home or in a public place. This impressed me! Since I knew people loved to identify publicly with a champion sports team, I figured that the religion which people most enthusiastically embraced *publicly* would probably contain the most truth. Christianity in America was basically a "private" matter. Islam in Turkey was public! I began to read the Koran, or more appropriately an English "interpretation" (it is not called a translation) of the Koran.

The war in Vietnam was a reality: most men my age were either in college or in the military. My parents and I were patriotic, but none of us was eager for me to be drafted. They wanted me to get a college education, then join the military if I desired. So I began looking for a college to attend. I chose the

University of Maryland branch campus located on a military base in Munich, Germany. It was a small two-year school of about two hundred students, primarily military and embassy dependents. I began classes in early 1967.

I do not know if there were any Christians on campus. There were about six of us who attended the Protestant chapel. None of us knew Jesus personally. Occasionally, about a dozen students attended Catholic mass. None of them knew Jesus either. I say this because all of these students were my friends—both before and after I was converted—and I knew them pretty well. Somewhat typical of college students of the late '60s, we partied a lot. (One international magazine stated that our campus had the highest per capita consumption of alcohol of any university in the world.)

Many students, however, did more than just drink. A few of us were fairly serious students. We did our homework, we studied for tests and exams, and we partied moderately most of the time. I was in this group. My main extracurricular activities were distance running and pinochle. During my second year at Munich, my partner and I won the pinochle championship for the entire school!

In the fall of 1967 our Protestant chaplain announced that the chapel wanted to sponsor a Friday-evening, all-day-Saturday retreat to Berchtesgaden in the Bavarian Alps. The package included skiing, hiking, and especially a chance to get off campus. In order to justify use of a military bus we needed more than our normal six students, so we advertised on campus and got nearly a bus load. A military dentist and his wife came as chaperones. Two American exchange students who were attending the University of Munich that year heard about the trip and also registered.

Shortly after our arrival, the chaplain surprised most of us. Since this was a religious retreat, we were going to have two meetings that evening, one for guys and one for gals. The leaders would be the two exchange students from the University of Munich.

Our leader introduced himself. His name was Ron Jensen, and besides being a student he was affiliated with an organization called Campus Crusade for Christ. (None of us from the University of Maryland had ever heard of it.) Ron said he wanted to share a verse from the Bible and talk about it. That got my attention because I could remember only a few times in my life when a minister had used the Bible as a basis for his message. Then when Ron stated that the verse was from the book of Revelation, I was *really* ready to pay attention! I had read in some magazine that approximately half of all mental patients had their problems caused by religion, and many of these problems occurred from trying to deal with the book of Revelation.

"Behold, I stand at the door, and knock: if any man hear my voice, and open the door, I will come in to him, and will sup with him, and he with me" (Revelation 3:20). After reading the verse—this statement by the Lord Jesus—Ron didn't ask us if we understood it. Instead, he looked directly at me and asked if I *believed* it. I answered that I did not. Why? Because with the possible exception of him (the chaplain and chaperone were not in the room) I was the best person in the room: I studied harder, drank less, didn't smoke or do drugs, and so far was sexually pure. Therefore, if Jesus would be in anyone's life He would be in mine, and He *wasn't*—so the verse was not true. Ron then asked if I had ever asked Jesus to come into my life. I answered that I had not. End of conversation. I have no recollection of anything else said in the room that evening.

The next day I hiked up the road from our lodge toward the "Eagle's Nest," Hitler's hideaway. It was a long hike, beginning on the lower slopes, going through the cloud layer, until I eventually came out above the clouds into a beautiful sunny sky. (I don't believe I had a single religious thought that day.)

Two months later, in late January of 1968, I was in a study room in my dorm reading a history book. All of a sudden Revelation 3:20 came back into my mind! With it came three questions:

Question one. Did I believe in God? I had been interested in science all my life and had studied evolution from a purely secular standpoint. However, the more I studied the more I became convinced that a self-starting and self-sustaining evolution was impossible. That left me with God as, at the very least, the starter of evolution. Yes, *there had to be a God.*

I may have been assisted toward a clear belief in God by two preconversion experiences. The first took place when I was in eighth or ninth grade. I was on a Boy Scout camporee at Fort Bragg, North Carolina. A camporee is a gathering of a number of scout troops for several days of camping and related events. I got up early one morning and went walking by myself through the pine forest that surrounded the camp area. The ground was covered with a layer of brown pine straw, and the trees were all tall, with the lowest branches several feet above my head.

Suddenly I entered a small clearing and found myself in a shaft of light. At the same time I heard organ music. I did not "feel" God, but I was aware of a wonderful sense of harmony, peace and order, and of a consciousness behind all this.

The second helpful experience occurred on the first day of English class in my tenth or eleventh grade at high school. The teacher told us all to close our eyes, think of God, and then tell the class what we "pictured." All the other students (except one who said he pictured nothing) spoke of majestic mountains, powerful waterfalls, vast forests, brilliant skies, and various other magnificent natural wonders. When I closed my eyes, however, I saw a pure soft white, and I felt warm and at peace. This white was not an emptiness but a clean, spotless fullness.

Question two. Did I believe Jesus to be the Son of God? I had heard Him called this all my life. However it may have been my study of Islam that caused the real impact in this regard. Although Muslims absolutely deny the divinity of Jesus, the *respect* many of them have for Him can exceed that of many "Christians." I realized that Jesus, the founder of Christianity and possibly the second most honored person in Islam, was certainly more than a mere man or teacher. Therefore I responded that yes, Jesus *is* the Son of God, whatever that means or implies.

Question three. Did I believe the Bible to be the Word of God? I had clearly been taught that it was not. However, in that instant I simply knew without any doubt or reservation that the Bible *is* the Word of God. Therefore

Revelation 3:20 had to be *true*—and Jesus would come into my life if I asked Him! Sitting in my chair, I simply asked Him to come in, and He *did*. There were no grand emotions or feelings, just an assurance that the Son of God is faithful to His word. I don't know the date. A little over a year later, when I came to know some people who noted their spiritual birthday, I chose January 28 because it was at least close.

Three essential questions—about God, Jesus Christ, and the Bible. And as they occurred to me, there in that study room, I was surely led step by step to the right answers and the proper action. What would you call this untaught understanding that contradicted my earlier teachings about the Bible? Was it the leading of an angel, or a miracle, or simply God at work?

•   •   •   •   •

I was not instantly transformed in all my thoughts and habits, but I did notice the initial change the next day. The first person who saw me in the classroom building that morning asked me, "What's new?" Without thinking, and with ease and joy, I replied, "I asked Jesus into my heart." I began thinking about God, praying while I ran. I began reading the Bible. I knew that since it is the Word of God, I am expected to know what it says and to live according to its precepts. And I hungered for that knowledge. That year I read through the entire Bible twice and the New Testament another two or three times.

Within a few days *substantial changes* were becoming obvious in my life. I wish I could say I continually went onward and upward with no slips, bumps, or mistakes (sins). It didn't happen that way, but the more I studied the Bible and got to know Jesus, the steadier my walk became. I also wish I could say that chapel attendance helped a lot too, but I still don't remember the Bible being used much in chapel. However, the military dentist—who was one of our chaperones on the trip—turned out to be a Christian who had had Campus Crusade for Christ and Navigators training. He heard about my conversion and invited me to his apartment. I spent several wonderful evenings with him and his wife. In addition, I saw Ron a couple of times after my conversion and got counsel and encouragement from him before he finished his exchange program and returned to America.

Chapter 2

A Lamb Among Wolves

W hat did *not* change after my conversion was my environment. To the best of my knowledge, I was the only Christian on campus. However, in God's goodness, He made the two semesters at U of M in the calendar year of 1968 a tremendously fertile field for my spiritual growth.

The first encouragement was many of my fellow students. They all heard about my conversion. A few of them mocked me, but most of them encouraged me. One of my friends said, "I used to be a Christian. Here are some things I was taught that may be helpful to you." They *were* helpful. Similar helps came through other students. They appreciated my sincerity and my intention to follow Christ.

The second encouragement came from a number of my professors, even the ones who were vocally antagonistic to religion. I'll share four brief stories.

I was taking Speech the semester I was converted. Our teacher said that if we wanted to be sure of getting an "A" for the class, we should enter the speech contest. Each contestant would have about seven minutes to speak before the entire student body. Between the time I entered and the date I gave my speech I became a Christian, so for my speech I decided to give my testimony. We had to write out our speech and present it to the instructor a week before the contest. After reading mine, he called me into his office. He was very upset and said my speech was totally inappropriate. He also shared how he had been reared as the son of a minister, so he "knew Christianity was not true." (I couldn't help wondering if some of his hostility was due to the fact that he was moonlighting as a bartender. Later, when I learned about the convicting power of the Word of God, I concluded my teacher had felt this conviction and was reacting *against* it rather than responding *to* it.) I reminded him that there had been no restriction as to the topic, so he agreed to let me give my speech as I had prepared it. I didn't win the contest, but I did get to explain to all the students how I had become a Christian. I also got an "A" for the course.

The next semester—my last in Munich—God used three classes to strengthen my faith. The first was Anthropology. The first day of class, the professor asked if any of us were

Christians. Four of us raised our hands. (I knew the other students well, and while they were religious I don't believe they had an understanding of the gospel.) The professor was delighted that some of us would be so foolish, and guaranteed that by the end of the term we would reject our silly faith. He did teach anthropology, but he also spent a lot of time explaining how early man was aware of his limitations, and so mankind made up the concept of God in order to give a higher justification for the moral demands society needed for survival. When the semester was over, if he had asked how many believed in God, I think half the class would have raised their hands because each of his arguments had sounded progressively more ridiculous.

The second useful class that semester was English Literature. We read several books, including Dante's *Inferno*, Homer's *Odyssey*, and one titled *The Bible as Literature*. We had to do a major term paper on some aspect of one of the books, so I did my paper on the book of Romans from the New Testament. I was delighted to spend hours studying the Bible for a school project.

Finally I had Introduction to Philosophy. I enjoyed the teacher. He questioned nearly every statement we made or idea we had. However, he never stated his own beliefs, so none of us knew where he stood. When it was time for the final exam, he told us we would have to choose one of two questions he would present and write our answer to that question. The question I selected was: "What is the controlling factor in the universe, and is this factor just?" I spent two hours filling my blue book, identifying God as the Creator and Controller, and declaring not only His justice but His mercy—which caused Him to send Jesus to take the punishment for our sins so that we might be forgiven.

For the events of that year I don't claim any miracles or angelic assistance, but God was certainly at work.

Chapter 3

Redirection

I mentioned that my conversion was in January of 1968. One morning in March of that year, I awoke in my dorm room with the certainty that God wanted me to be a minister. I was not delighted. At that time I was planning to major in Forestry in order to get a job either in Alaska or Colorado, where I had lived, or possibly in Montana. I wanted to be far from people in general because I did not like people.

As I related earlier, I was born into a military family. As a result of my father's profession and professionalism I had a deep respect for authority. Yet at the time of my conversion I did not consciously acknowledge Jesus as my Lord. This was mainly because I was accustomed to hearing the word "Lord" used in vulgar or profane expressions. However, I did have an instant understanding that Jesus was my Commander-in-chief—much as the Philippian jailer in Acts 16 understood Christ's jurisdiction.

Therefore I could not disobey God, nor could I argue with Him. I could, in all sincerity, tell Him that I was sure I was misunderstanding Him. Surely one of the qualifications for entering the ministry was to *like people!* God simply ignored my claim of misunderstanding His directive. In fact, we had no communication at all. I prayed and . . . nothing. After about two weeks I finally said, "God, I don't understand this at all. I think you want me to be a minister, and I feel I am unqualified because of my feelings about people. However, if that is what You really want, I will do it." Immediately I could tell the lines of communication were open and clear.

Within two or three days I realized God was changing me. I found I not only liked my fellow students and professors, I loved them. The Father taught me a principle—when He directs, I obey. Enabling does not precede obedience, it follows or accompanies obedience. In other words, God wants us to take faith steps.

Later that year I took the next step. I knew ministers went to "religious" schools. I knew of one in North Carolina because I had attended church camp there for one week one summer. (I can't remember many overtly religious activities at the camp, but that did not seem important.) I applied to the school and was accepted to start classes sometime after Christmas in 1969.

However, shortly before finishing my sophomore year at Munich and heading home to Turkey, I had received an application from Asbury College in Kentucky. I had never heard of Asbury College, and the only recollection I had of Kentucky was twisting roads through mountains, a crummy restaurant, and stories about Daniel Boone (a very distant relative). I stuck the application deep in my suitcase.

About the same time, in my regular Bible reading I came to Psalm 32 and was strongly impressed by verse eight, "I will instruct thee and teach thee in the way which thou shalt go: I will guide thee with mine eye." (You may have noticed that I used the King James Version here and for Revelation 3:20 earlier; it's because I had a KJV Bible when I came to Christ. It is what I read most of the time for the first years of my Christian life, and my initial memorization was all from the King James. When I returned from Africa in 1980, I began using the New International Version because it was the common text on most college campuses. But these events in my life happened in King James terms, and it seems most accurate to refer back to it.)

I knew that God had every right to direct my life. He had already done that by calling me into the ministry. Now I began pondering the idea of seeking direction. For example, was the application from Asbury College God's idea? I returned to Turkey with that question unanswered. So I began seeking advice from others. First I asked my parents. My father was unhappy to hear about any kind of ministerial preparation, so he wanted nothing to do with any conversation about spiritual guidance. My mother was strongly in favor of the school in North Carolina. It was near where she and my father were due to go in eighteen months for his terminal assignment in the military. I would be close to home and able to visit on most weekends. Also, the school had ties with the denomination to which Mom and I belonged, so it was almost certain I would receive a scholarship.

My mother's final argument was her strongest: the war in Vietnam was bigger than before, and there was no way I would have time to apply to Asbury and be accepted before the next term, so I had to choose between the school in North Carolina or the military. If I didn't join I would be drafted. As I prayed, however, I felt more and more strongly about Asbury.

I made a deal with Mom. I would apply to Asbury, and if I did not receive my acceptance within two weeks, I would go to the other school. She was ecstatic. I had to write from Turkey to Germany to have my college transcripts sent to Kentucky; I had to write from Turkey to Colorado to have my high school transcripts sent. She knew there was no way I would hear within two weeks. Amazingly, it took ten days! I was going to Asbury College.

At that time in my life I knew six Christians. I have since inquired of every one of them if he or she was the person who asked Asbury to send me an application. Asbury does *not* send unsolicited applications to sophomores in other colleges. All six said they were *not involved.* Was it an angel, a miracle, or simply God at work?

Chapter 4

The Power of
Corporate Prayer

Within a week of my arrival at Asbury College I had another spiritual lesson. I was living on the third floor of Johnson East dormitory. One day I saw a note posted on the bathroom door announcing a hall prayer meeting that evening. After I arrived I found it was not mandatory, but I wanted to be there. Actually, I had never before been in a group prayer meeting.

After introductions and general conversation, the leader asked if anyone had any prayer requests. There was a time of silence, so I asked, "What do you mean by a prayer request?" Boy, was I a rookie! He explained that it was something for which I had a special desire to pray. I took a letter from my mother from my pocket and read to the guys about Mrs. Benny, a friend of the family. She had been on an airplane from Turkey to Greece when something happened to the pressurization in the plane. Her eardrums had ruptured and she couldn't hear. "Could that be a prayer request?" I inquired. He said yes, and asked how I wanted them to pray. I thought it seemed good to ask that her hearing be restored. That's what we asked. A few days later I got another letter from Mom. In it she mentioned that Mrs. Benny's hearing had suddenly returned!

I shared that at the next hall meeting. Corporate prayer was fun!

My first Sunday at Asbury I went to a Baptist church just off campus. I had no real denominational understanding, but my grandmother (Mom's side) was perhaps the most godly person I had known and she was Baptist. During the next week a group of students invited me to go with them to a mission work in the poorer area of Nicholas-ville, a nearby town. That week we did street ministry, jail ministry, and held services in the mission itself. That was the end of my traditional church attendance while at college. For about eighteen months I was part of a team of students ministering at Nicholasville two or three days per week in a variety of ministries.

Before almost every meeting we met as a group to pray for the town, for the mission, for individuals, and of course for ourselves. As we prayed together we became increasingly bold in our prayers—not in arrogance, but in faith. We saw many answers to our prayers in terms of people listening to us outdoors, in terms of people coming to the mission, and in terms of people praying to receive Christ.

One day a group of us went to a park where a number of black teens were playing basketball or just lounging. We played some basketball, played our guitars, sang, and shared testimonies. Later a few of these same teens came to the mission. We heard later that this park was strictly black turf, totally off-limits to whites. We could have been beaten or worse, and had our guitars smashed. We felt God specifically answered our bold prayers.

Early in the fall of 1969, a group of six guys (four of us from the college and two from Asbury Theological Seminary) began meeting each evening, Monday through Saturday, for an hour of prayer. We soon decided we wanted more time together, so we added an hour at noon each day and fasted through lunch while we prayed. Soon after that we decided that in addition to all six of us fasting each of the six days at lunch, one of us would fast *all* day on a specific day.

Of the two hours together, we spent about thirty minutes talking and discussing our prayer requests and about ninety minutes in prayer. As we listened to one another, we found our faith and expectations growing. We didn't advertise, but others (girlfriends, for example) knew of our group and sent us prayer requests. We found ourselves praying specifically and getting specific answers.

The highlight was one Tuesday morning near the end of the term when three of us at the college, without consultation, asked our professors in our eight and nine o'clock classes if we could pray as a class that day for revival. We did. At ten o'clock we had chapel, and at the end of chapel an altar call was given for anyone who felt he or she needed to do business with God. Within a couple of minutes nearly one hundred of the eleven hundred students had gone to the front of the auditorium, filling the altar and all the available floor space. Was such a specific answer the work of an angel, a miracle, or simply God at work?

•   •   •   •   •

At the end of that term our group disbanded. Most of us joined or started other prayer groups on campus. I have no idea how many of the students at Asbury were involved in college-sponsored and unsponsored prayer meetings. Most of my friends were! It was shortly afterwards, on February 3, 1970, when one of the famous Asbury revivals began. (That is a separate story of God's sovereignty and majesty. You can obtain a copy of *One Divine Moment*, edited by Dr. Robert E. Coleman, through the Asbury College bookstore, Wilmore, KY 40390.)

Shortly after the 1970 Asbury revival began, the student body was in chapel (the initial chapel service lasted seven days and seven nights) when one of the professors shared a prayer request from a hospital in nearby Lexington, Kentucky. A very small child had been severely burned and seemed to be dying. The doctor told the parents the hospital staff was doing all they could do, but he was not optimistic. He then told them he heard that out at Asbury College "something was happening: the students and teachers were praying, and God seemed to be doing whatever they asked." The parents called and asked us to pray for their baby. We did, hundreds of us together. The next day we received a report through the hospital that shortly after we prayed, the child seemed to receive a surge of strength and actually sat up and held and drank from a bottle.

•   •   •   •   •

Now let me fast-forward a few years. Linda and I were married in 1972. During the years 1976-1979 we served as church planters with WEC International in Guinea-Bissau, West Africa, and consistently saw the power of corporate prayer.

Many of those who came to Christ from

animistic or Muslim backgrounds faced some level of persecution, generally from their family. Good wishes from their fellow Christians were not adequate. These children of Christ needed *protection* and *provision*.

Though we prayed together at every service, we soon saw a need to have an extended prayer meeting on each Saturday. The meeting lasted about three hours. After a five-to-ten-minute devotional to focus our attention and encourage our faith, we simply presented urgent prayer requests and prayed until we were confident as a group that God had heard our prayers and would give the answer that would glorify Him. We generally prayed for only two or three issues during the three hours, but as each person prayed—once, twice, perhaps more often for each matter— our corporate faith grew. Then we would "corporately" sense God had answered and we were free to move to another topic. We prayed for housing for someone kicked out of his home. We prayed for safety for one called to return to his home village where he would have to publicly deny his tribal religion. We prayed about a lot of illnesses, since Guinea-Bissau at that time was the unhealthiest country in the world. We had many requests and many answers. We did not get the answer we desired for *every* prayer we prayed, but we got so many that we were encouraged to ask *more* and *more* of God—so that the tribes among whom we lived would be forced to acknowledge Him.

While we occasionally had some major prayer battles, our main teaching besides asking *specifically* was to ask in *simplicity.* Most of the prayer requests during our regular church meetings were brief and specific.

After we moved from the capital city of Bissau to Bafata and began our first church, Linda and I engaged mainly in evangelism and basic teaching. People rarely visited our church prior to conversion because it was risky politically, since Guinea-Bissau was Marxist at the time. It was risky also because we were opposed by both Muslims and animists, since the gospel message contradicted their teachings. Our evangelism therefore took place outdoors and house-to-house, while our church meetings for the first year were very basic instruction for *new believers* as God won them to Himself. Part of this instruction was prayer by example, and then learning prayer by praying.

One Sunday morning I had planned to teach on "anointing the sick" as taught by James. That morning our daughter, Becky, about two years old at the time, awoke with a very high fever. As she slumped on Linda's lap in our small 12- by 14-foot church room, the six or so other believers could almost feel the heat pouring from Becky's body. (In case you wonder why we would take Becky to church when she was sick, our first church was a room in our house. It was quite convenient, and both Linda and I could keep an eye on Becky.) I knew God wanted me to continue with the planned message. After talking about sickness and giving various examples from the Bible, I read the text from James and simply said I would demonstrate on Becky. (I wish I could say I had nothing but perfect faith, but I was nervous because this was the first anointing in the Bafata church.) In God's goodness, as soon as Becky was anointed she sat up and the fever was gone. This provoked a lot of discussion. When an animist or Muslim went to his local witch doctor, the procedure involved ceremonies for discernment of cause, followed by the determination of what charms or additional ceremonies the family would have to purchase and perform, and then the actually doing of what was required. Our believers were *astounded* that God did His work for *free* and so easily!

Here is another example: Eusébio was from the pagan Balanta tribe. He came to our home to receive Christ as a result of our outdoor evangelism. A few weeks later, I was called by one of his unsaved family members to come to their home. Eusébio was lying on a bamboo mat on the floor in the rear of their tin-roof mud-brick house. They told me he did not want any tribal ceremonies, but I was supposed to pray for him in the name of Jesus. The entire family gathered around as I prayed for him. Nothing seemed to happen, and I had nothing additional to say. After encouraging Eusébio, I turned to leave the room and the family followed me to the front door. When I was a few yards down the dirt road, however, they turned around, and Eusébio was standing behind them, totally well.

A few months later one of our other believers was ill, but Linda and I were out of town, so he called for Eusébio to pray for him. Eusébio prayed for him and he was instantly well. The message was obvious. We did not need specially trained and highly paid healers. God hears the prayer of any of those who believe Him.

God did not answer *every* prayer for healing with healing, but He did so about seventy percent of the time. We decided not to try to explain the thirty percent as being due to lack of faith, unconfessed sin, or anything else—God knew why! We decided to be encouraged by the seventy percent and keep asking.

The third church Linda and I planted was in the small town of Bambadinka. When we first went there to do evangelism we found that God had gone before us. António and Guiterria were already there. They had been converted years earlier in another part of the country and were sent to Bambadinka because António had a government job.

They had maintained their faith, although they were generally very discreet because of the many pressures they faced. When Linda and I arrived in town they heard of our arrival, invited us to their home, and asked us to come weekly to hold meetings at their home.

A few weeks later Adolfo and Quinta came to a meeting. Quinta had given birth to at least ten children, but only three were alive. Adolfo worked with António, who had begun to witness to him about the power of God. Adolfo and Quinta soon came to the Lord, and both couples got together regularly for prayer and fellowship. At one of these meetings Anna was with them. She and her husband were interested in the gospel but were as yet unconvinced. That afternoon she had her only child with her, a two-year-old girl who had never walked. As the two couples talked about God, Anna asked if the God of the Bible could do "anything." They said He could. She then asked if He could make her daughter walk. They answered that He could if He chose, and the way to find out if He was willing was to *ask*. So they simply asked God to help Anna's little girl walk. When Anna's husband returned home later that afternoon, his little girl ran to him. He was at the next meeting. An angel, a miracle, or simply God at work?

•   •   •   •   •

The Bible tells us that where two or three are gathered in Jesus' name, He is there (Matthew 18:20). It also tells us that when even two ask, He answers (Matthew 18:19). But this is not meant to discredit individual prayers, because we are also commanded to pray privately—in our closet (Matthew 6:6). However, we have many examples in Scripture of answered corporate prayer.

There is another strength to corporate prayer that most of us thankfully do not have to experience. After a year or so in Bafata, I found I could not pray privately; I would go to sleep, even if I was standing. I made sure I was getting enough rest and eating as well as possible in that extremely poor country. Linda and I finally determined that the attack was spiritual, and so we used our traditional missionary prayer letter to ask people to pray for me so that I could pray. (This was occurring at the same time as many of our most successful Saturday corporate prayer meetings. God was using the corporate prayers to sustain me in my time of personal struggle.) After several weeks, I could pray privately standing with my eyes open; then with my eyes closed; then sitting, then kneeling; then in any position I wished.

My private time with God is precious. It is there, I believe, that I come to know Him more and more. Yet it seems to be through *corporate* prayer that He especially manifests Himself to both believers and unbelievers. It is when I am praying among others that I seem to have the faith to pray what I call "God-sized" prayers.

In the twenty years that Linda and I have been on the home staff of WEC, located near Philadelphia, we have been involved in at least a thousand corporate prayer meetings. Again and again we feel God has shown a simple pattern: *Asking together* leads to *believing together* which leads to *receiving together*.

Do we need miracles in order to believe in corporate prayer? I don't think so. My experience is that regular corporate prayer produces results that stimulate faith, which then encourages more prayer. *Doing* brings results which motivate *more* doing. It may be simple acts of God, but we will be encouraged as if we were seeing miracles. Maybe we are!

Chapter 5

Guidance:
Two Steps Forward

In chapter three I shared how God guided me to Asbury College to prepare for the ministry. I still have no idea how God got the application for Asbury to me, and I am still astounded that I received the acceptance so quickly. Is this the normal pattern for guidance? Not in *my* life. However, I am not sure I know what a "normal" pattern is. While the leading to Asbury may have been somewhat dramatic, the leading into ministry was absolutely matter-of-fact. I'd like to share several stories of how God led Linda and me and let you draw your own conclusions.

I had been at Asbury just a few weeks when I met Linda Kellermicr, a freshman from Ohio. Neither of us knows exactly when or how we met. I spent a lot of time with a group of guys and she with a group of girls. Since our two groups spent a good bit of time together, we think that during one of these times we actually "met." Two or three people claim to have introduced us. (They each would like to take some of the credit, we think, for our good marriage.)

There seems to have been nothing unusual about Linda getting to Asbury. She graduated from high school in Steubenville, Ohio, with good grades and the desire to train to be an elementary school teacher. She loved Jesus and wanted to train at a Christian college. Her father had attended Asbury briefly, and she had an uncle who had graduated from there. The Elementary Education program was very good. Since Asbury met her requirements she applied, but she was initially turned down because of a positive TB tine-test. Her older brother had had tuberculosis so she had been exposed at least through him. Several x-rays and a strong letter from Linda's family doctor convinced the Asbury administration that she was "inactive" and in no way infectious, so she began her studies in the fall of 1968. In short, Linda's guidance seems to be a common example of a godly interest, an acceptable option, and a little perseverance.

We started dating and soon decided to become a bit more serious. We traded high school class rings. I put hers on my right pinkie. After she wrapped several layers of yarn around mine she put it on her right ring finger. Wonderful! However, the night after we traded rings was one of the worst I can remember. I had the strongest feeling that this was wrong and that I needed to ask Linda to return my ring and take hers back, possibly ending our relationship. Yet I knew I had prayed *before* suggesting the initial exchange and had felt very positive. What had gone wrong?

As I prayed that night, three possibilities presented themselves. First, I had absolutely misunderstood God and had acted on my own impulse. He did not want us to be serious about each other and perhaps not even to be dating. The second possibility was what I call an "Isaac" scenario: It was God who gave Isaac to Abraham and then told him to present his son as a sacrifice; God did not want Isaac killed, but Abraham did not know this until he was stopped by God in the act of sacrificing him. In the same way, perhaps God did not want us to end our relationship but He wanted to know that we were *willing* to do this for Him. The third situation: it could be Satan trying to make me think he was God because he was afraid of the ministry potential Linda and I might have together. I asked God to show me which of these was the truth. But no answer came.

The next morning I had an idea. Linda and I generally met in the library around six-thirty p.m. to study. (I told you earlier *I* was a serious student. So was *she*.) I prayed and told the Lord that I would go to the library at six-twenty. If Linda was there, I would tell her that I knew we were supposed to go our separate ways. But if she wasn't there, I would wait there until six-forty. *She had to come within those twenty minutes or we were through*. I went to the library, and she hadn't come. I sat in a chair facing the entrance. I noticed a clock above the door, a clock that made an audible click as the minute hand jumped from one minute to the next. Linda came up the steps. As her foot crossed the threshold of the entrance the clock jumped to six-thirty. I shared with her what had happened. She told me she had actually started toward the library at about six o'clock, but one of the girls on her dorm floor had stopped her because she had to talk to her "right now."

An angel, a miracle, or simply God at work?

• • • • •

As I approached the summer of 1969 I needed a summer job. I needed a *good* job to earn a lot of money. My father had offered to help pay my way through Asbury, but I had declined his help because I really felt that God wanted Dad to see *Him* put me through— to help draw my father toward faith in Jesus. I couldn't go home to get a job because my parents were still in Turkey. So I asked God for a job. I told him I really did not want to look myself, since I was a little concerned as a new Christian that I might miss His will. Therefore, would He please bring the job to me, and I needed one to earn enough for a full year of college.

A few days later Lincoln Stevens, a fellow student, asked me if I had a summer job, and if not, would I go with him for an interview. Since I had nothing, I went. I was surprised when the man we went to see showed me a set of three Bible reference books. I looked at them and wanted to buy them. Then he told me he was with the Southwestern Company out of Nashville, Tennessee, and he wanted me to sell the books for the summer. I would get a commission. This seemed to be my answer and I was at peace, so I agreed instantly. After sales school in Nashville I was part of a team of three assigned to the Parkersburg, West Virginia, area.

I was not a good salesman in terms of doing things just right. I knew my sales pitch, but instead of moving rapidly from house to house after presentations I often spent time with those who placed an order. I was able to share my faith with several people, and a good number gave me excellent help in my Christian walk. Well, despite my poor technique I turned out to be the second best salesman in the

state of West Virginia, and was in the top
thirty in the entire division of the company
that summer! I earned enough for my tuition
for the next year. God had guided and provided
as a seal of His guidance.

I had not applied for a job at Asbury. I
figured I needed the time to study and I also
assumed there was no way to get a job since
so many students had applied. But one day I
was asked if I would please come and work in
the kitchen. One of the student breakfast cooks
had quit and they needed another. No one, it
seems, wanted to come in early to cook for
maybe three hundred students. One of the
guys in my dorm who turned down the job
told the cafeteria manager about me—"some
character who was always up by five a.m." So
I was asked to take the job, and I did. I had to
get up a little earlier for my personal devo-
tions, but that was no problem. I now had
money for special things, like dating Linda
and buying books. In this case the guidance
came solely through *others*. I was the answer
to *their* need.

As the summer of 1970 approached I was
asked by Southwestern to sell books again, as
a crew leader. I would recruit students as
Lincoln had recruited me. I would sell and
earn a commission, and I would earn a commission from every recruit. I clearly felt God
telling me to refuse the job.

I was a trained and experienced lifeguard; I had also recently been certified as a Water Safety Instructor. I got job offers in this area from New Jersey and Colorado. Again God said no. As I asked God for wisdom, I felt I should be with my parents. They had recently moved to North Carolina. It had been sixteen months since I had seen them. I caught a bus to Fayetteville and had a great couple of weeks at home. I got more job offers there but again had no peace about taking any of them.

After two weeks at home I got a call from Bob Odom, one of my former prayer-team partners at Asbury. He was now a student pastor in Ohio, and he told me of a pastor friend who was responsible for a lot of little churches. He was looking for someone to preach at two of these for the summer or to be the youth program-coordinator for several of them. I prayed, packed, and took a bus to Ohio. But the pastor for whom I expected to work met me and told me he had changed his mind. I could stay with him for a night or two and then go back to North Carolina if I wanted. He did not ask me if I had money for a bus ticket—which I did not—nor did he offer to reimburse me for the ticket I had purchased. Bob heard what happened and invited me to join him and his wife at their parsonage. I gladly accepted.

Bob presented me with another option.

Camp Tarhe (named after an Indian) was a small Christian camp to which several area pastors sent their church kids. It was primitive and very inexpensive. Campers paid five dollars per week if they had the money and went for free if they didn't. The staff consisted of unpaid volunteers. If I went there I wouldn't get a salary, but I would get experience. Again I prayed and felt it was right, so I went. "Primitive" was a very good description. Bathrooms were outhouses and the bathing facility was the creek. I loved it!

I arrived a week before camp and helped get things ready. During the two weeks of camp I served as a dorm monitor, lifeguard, trash emptier, and general laborer. One of my jobs in the dorm was to ascertain the spiritual state of each of the twelve to fifteen boys and see how I could help them. That summer I was allowed to lead several of these boys to the Lord. Several more accepted Christ during the daytime classes or evening meetings. By the end of each week everyone in my cabin professed to know Jesus, and it was the same in most of the other cabins. It was a great ministry environment.

Financially, it looked to be a disaster; but I was too busy to worry much. I certainly didn't tell anyone I needed money. How could I explain why I was working as a volunteer instead of looking for a paying job? Early in

the first week of camp one of the other staff
members handed me twenty dollars, telling
me God told her to do it. I was baffled and
offered it back because God had not told me
to take it. She laughed and said I had to keep
it, so I did. Several other people gave me
money, to the point of several hundred dollars.

After camp I stayed on a few more weeks
to help with cleanup and general maintenance.
I had a dorm to myself and all the food I
could eat. I was also invited to preach at a
couple of churches and was surprised to find
that I was paid to do so. The money accumulated, but it wouldn't get me through
Asbury.

Near the end of the summer one couple
approached me. He was a manager at a local
plant and she had been our camp nurse. They
said they felt strange, but it seemed God was
moving them to give me some money, although
they knew I didn't need any since I had never
said anything. Could they help me? I needed
about five hundred dollars more; I was
embarrassed, however, to say anything over
one hundred. As I was about to speak, they
said they really felt five hundred dollars was
what they should give. Was that okay?

That summer I had worked for free, had
gained valuable ministry experience, and had
obtained the money I needed for school. But I
had not done what I went to Ohio to do! What

was wrong with the guidance? Nothing. I learned that sometimes God gets us to point A in order to give us the information to get us to point B or beyond. Guidance is God's responsibility; following is mine.

•   •   •   •   •

I returned to Asbury. When I had begun my studies there was no specific course that was strictly for ministerial preparation since Asbury is a Christian Liberal Arts college. So I chose to major in Philosophy and Religion. This way I got more Bible than in any other major. But in the fall of 1970 a Bible major was added. I was planning to graduate in February or March, whenever the winter quarter ended; now if I could stay one more quarter and took maximum loads both quarters, I could graduate in June with my class and have a double major. I would need more money, but only by the time the second quarter began. This time I asked for and got a job at school. What about loans and grants and scholarships? For some unknown reason, the school never sent me information about such financial resources, so until the last quarter of my senior year I never knew I could borrow or request money.

A couple of weeks after school began the director of Camp Tarhe contacted me. He was also the pastor of a circuit of four small United Methodist churches. He had the opportunity to take one larger church, which would be easier on him and his family since balancing camp and four churches was difficult. He asked if I would accept a student pastorate for the four churches he was leaving. I prayed and told him that if he could get approval for me from his superiors I would be glad to. He got the permission with two conditions. I had to be a member of a United Methodist church and be approved as a ministerial student.

Wilmore, Kentucky, is the home of the First Methodist Church, one of finest and most evangelical churches of any kind anywhere. I had been there for various Asbury-related evangelistic services. Dr. David Seamands was pastor. I met with him and explained that I would like to join his church and never attend. He asked why, and I explained I was the team leader for Nicholasville mission and wanted to become a student pastor for four Methodist churches in Ohio, 130 miles to the north. He thought that was reasonable; so I became a United Methodist pastor for my senior year at Asbury College, for my one year at Asbury Seminary while I waited for Linda to graduate from college, and for the first year of our marriage. And again the Lord provided. Even though I had to buy a car and rent my own parsonage, the salary from the churches covered the balance I needed to pay for my extra time at college. Since I had always tried to carry heavy study loads—because I wanted to learn all I could—I was able to graduate with nearly five years' worth of credits. Every course has been valuable to me. I spent my weekdays in Kentucky as a student and my weekends in Ohio as a pastor. God had guided and He had provided.

· · · · ·

While at Asbury I read a lot of books for class, but I also read 400 to 500 pages per week for personal development and relaxation. One of the books I read was about George Müller, a German minister called to move to England to establish orphanages. The unique aspect of his ministry was that God led him to never make his financial needs known to anyone outside the organization. Before he began the orphanages he was a pastor. It was there that God started him in the life of faith. He told the church he was pastoring that he did not want a salary. Instead he would receive love gifts and live off them. If he could not live off their love, he did not want to live off their salary. After my first year in the pastorate I felt I should ask my churches to do the same with me. I wasn't sure why, but it seemed important. All four churches agreed.

In one of the four I began to receive more money; in another I received less. The other two said they would accept my wish to live by faith, but they made sure their love gifts matched my former salary to the penny. Bless them for their compassion toward their "crazy-kid" pastor.

Earlier in my reading God brought three books my way in quick succession from three sources. The first was *C. T. Studd* by Norman Grubb. The second was *God's Smuggler* by Brother Andrew. The third was *Give Me This Mountain* by Dr. Helen Roseveare. Each of these is a missions book. C. T. Studd was the son of a wealthy Englishman won to Jesus by Dwight L. Moody. C.T. was considered the finest university athlete of his time. Yet after he came to Jesus, largely through the prayers and efforts of his father, God led him to leave everything and go to China. When his father died, God led him to give away all his inheritance and trust God after the pattern of George Müller. Studd eventually went to Africa and became the founder of WEC International.

"Brother Andrew" is the name used by a Dutchman who has committed his life to getting Scriptures and relief supplies to Christians in the most difficult countries in the world. After getting his Bible and missionary training at the WEC Missionary

Training College in Scotland, he eventually founded Open Doors, believing that God can open a door for His Word to be taken into any country. *God's Smuggler* is his testimony of God's provision, a true classic on living by faith.

Dr. Helen Roseveare trained in England to be a physician. After her conversion while a student at Cambridge University, she went as a medical missionary to the Belgian Congo with WEC. She writes about how God continued to work in her life even after she became a missionary, and through her nearly twenty years in Africa. Again, her policy was to trust God for all she needed, not merely for herself, but for all that was necessary to build, equip, and operate a hospital and nursing school.

After reading the book about C. T. Studd and the book by Brother Andrew, I had decided there was no way *I* could be a missionary. These two men seemed to be *giants* of faith and perseverance.

But as I read Dr. Roseveare's book, I realized I actually *could* be a missionary. I looked at myself analytically. So much of my life came together: I had, to my knowledge, never clearly heard the gospel until I was in college; though I had never embraced Islam I had seriously studied it; I had also seen the effect of Islam in Turkey. I realized that most

Muslims there and elsewhere would live and die without ever meeting a Christian, much less having the gospel presented to them. I had also been impressed by Romans 15:20 in which Paul declared that he sought to preach the gospel where it had never been preached. As a result, I began to ask God if I could do the same.

Was this a missionary "call"? I don't know. I didn't think God was telling me I *had* to be a missionary! But I did believe the call to ministry he had given me in 1968 could be fulfilled by being a missionary to an unreached people as well as by being a pastor in America. God certainly gave me the *interest* to do this; so I asked Him for the privilege of taking the gospel where no Christian had ever been.

It was shortly after this that I came across a leaflet by WEC in which it stated that in Portuguese Guinea (now Guinea-Bissau) there were two Muslim tribes that had never had a Christian witness among them. I felt that God was saying yes, and showing me where He would allow me to serve. I showed this to Linda, my fiancée, and she was in agreement.

We then had to find out where in the world Portuguese Guinea was. It is on the western coast of Africa. While Linda had never lived "by faith," she was a woman of faith who found it easy to say yes to God. We simply assumed we would serve with WEC, so we began the application process—although we knew we would not be ready to go for about two years. At this point, guidance was coming quietly and undramatically, but clearly. We felt we were taking two steps forward without any steps backward.

By this time I had asked Linda to marry me and she had agreed. We had seen many of our friends become engaged. Some had continued into marriage and others had broken their engagements. We knew this was a commitment to be taken seriously. During my first year at Asbury I had heard some of the guys telling how God told them they should marry a certain girl. This seemed quite within the bounds of appropriate guidance, so when I realized I was definitely in love with Linda, I asked God if I should marry her. I got a very clear answer: "If you want." That surprised me, so I continued to ask, and continued to get the same answer. When I finally took time to consider, I realized what a wonderful answer it was! This meant that God approved of me marrying, and that Linda fit all the qualifications of the godly woman I should seek. Therefore I would marry her because I *wanted* to, because I *loved* her. It also meant that if things got difficult I would have to remember that this was *my* desire, and I would have to choose to continue to be faithful and loving. Along with choice came *commitment* and *responsibility*; I could never tell God this was His fault. I told Linda what I had been praying and that God had given me permission to ask her. She shared how she had also been praying, asking God if she should marry me if I asked, and God had told her, "If you want." We wanted, and were married in her home church in Steubenville, Ohio, on July 22, 1972.

Chapter **6**

Guidance:
Faith in Our Father

Neither Linda nor I had much money when we married. I was earning just enough pastoring the four churches to maintain myself and my car and pay the rent on the parsonage. Linda had less, since after graduation she returned home to prepare for the wedding. Her parents paid for most of the wedding expenses and my parents provided a honeymoon place for a week on the North Carolina coast. As soon as the honeymoon was over, we planned to return to Ohio to try to arrange a job interview for Linda with the school district where I pastored. We really wanted her to have a year or two to use the teaching skills she had learned. We were confident they would be tremendously beneficial in Portuguese Guinea.

One evening as we opened the door to leave our apartment for a walk on the beach we met a highway patrolman with his hand raised to knock on the door. He had a simple message for us. We were to call my father. There was no phone in our apartment, and only a couple of pay phones on the public areas of the beach. We found one, phoned Dad, and learned what God had done.

Phyllis, a lady in one of my churches, was a school teacher and had heard about a couple of openings available in the district. This was a mainly rural community, so most teachers got jobs not by having their name in the district files but by hearing about such openings and calling to arrange interviews.

Linda's parents had left for vacation the day after our wedding. They needed it. Phyllis and her family had been invited to our wedding but were unable to come. She kept the invitation which had Linda's parents' address. Through directory assistance she got their number and called them to try to get a message to us. They were gone. However, Linda's aunt checked the house daily and "happened" to be there when the phone rang. She had already decided not to answer the phone if it did ring, because she didn't want to advertise that Linda's parents were away; their house was not in sight of any other house so it would be an ideal target for robbery. She changed her mind and answered the phone. No, she did not know how to contact us or Linda's parents. She did know where my parents had stayed, so she took the message from Phyllis and called the couple who had hosted my parents. Yes, they had exchanged addresses and phone numbers. Linda's aunt then called my parents, who were the ones who had provided the honeymoon hideaway for us. They knew there was no phone, but they contacted the highway patrol and gave them the physical address. Thus the patrolman at the door. We called my parents and then Phyllis. The next day Linda called the office of the superintendent to set up a job interview as soon as we got back from our honeymoon.

The morning of the interview the principal who was supposed to conduct the interviews was out of town, so Dr. Rogers, the school superintendent, took his place. After introductions Linda told Dr. Rogers that she was looking for a position for one or two years. He told her that this would prejudice the interview because the school wanted a career teacher. Why was she not looking for a career position? She shared how we were preparing to go to Africa as missionaries, that I was pastoring four churches nearby, and that she wanted to get experience as a teacher to help her prepare for what she anticipated doing overseas. Dr. Rogers said that fifteen teachers had applied for the position, but Linda was the first to be interviewed *and* the job was hers! He too was a Christian. God had certainly used a number of people who were in just the right place at just the right time to allow Linda to become a third grade teacher at Minford Elementary School in Minford, Ohio. Angels, miracles, or simply God at work?

•   •   •   •   •

Linda taught third grade for two years. Then she resigned her position because we knew it was time to begin our missionary career. In September 1974 we arrived at the WEC headquarters near Philadelphia, Pennsylvania, for the Candidate Orientation Course. We knew God was calling us to work with Muslims in Portuguese Guinea, which at that time was in the process of changing its name to Guinea-Bissau.

Portuguese Guinea had been a colony of Portugal for approximately five hundred years. In 1961 a group of men started a movement for independence that became a war much like the American Revolutionary War in the 1770s. By 1974 the Portuguese were tired of the war, so they granted their former colony independence. As a newly independent country, it needed a new name. Its people maintained the "Guinea" and added "Bissau," basically indicating that the country is the Guinea whose capital is Bissau. (Immediately to the south is the Republic of Guinea, which

had been a French colony. Its capital is
Conakry, so the people of Guinea-Bissau
generally call it Guinea-Conakry.)

The Portuguese had opposed Protestant
missionary work. In fact, no Protestant worker
had been allowed into the country until 1940
when the Portuguese allowed a single WEC
woman missionary to enter. That feat is a
long and complicated story, but suffice it to
say that this opened the door for WEC—
although there was often overt and covert
opposition to the work of the mission and the
national church. WEC was the only Protestant
mission in the country.

The mission was not sure independence
would bring any improvement to the situation.
The new government was Marxist; there was
no guarantee the mission would be allowed to
stay in the country. But, fortunately, it seemed
the new government was well aware of the
opposition of the Portuguese to the mission
and the church. The mission had established
medical, midwifery, and agricultural projects
which had benefited the people, so we had
some popular support. The government decided
WEC could stay, at least for a while.

Linda and I completed the four-month
Candidate Orientation Course, took some
initial Portuguese language study through
Berlitz while we waited for our first child to
be born, and then headed to Portugal for

additional studies. In January of 1976 we arrived in Guinea-Bissau.

Would we be allowed to move into the eastern half of Guinea-Bissau, the Muslim half? The Portuguese had never allowed a missionary to be there. Would the new Marxist government?

The Muslims were not pleased with the Marxist position of the new government. They too had fought for independence, so they basically told the government that if it tried to force atheism as an official policy, the Muslims would secede and perhaps join Senegal, a much larger and predominantly Muslim country to the north. The government was forced to say that it believed in freedom of religion, though it worked to teach atheism in the public schools and through the media. Still, the officially recorded position was freedom of religion.

Therefore, with the assistance of our field leader Gene McBride, we began seeking government permission for a move to Bafata, the "Muslim capital," and the second largest city in the country after Bissau itself. One of the arguments presented was that if they wanted to convince the Muslims that they really believed in freedom of religion, it could be illustrated by allowing us to move into the Muslim half of the country. We were given permission.

The second step was to get permission from the Muslim governor in Bafata. When we approached him, the only real question he had for me was whether or not I believed in God. I assured him that I did. His response was that they wanted anyone who believed in God to help against the atheistic teaching of the Marxists. He too granted permission. This may be the only known case in which Muslims and Marxists, working against each other, purposely allowed an evangelical ministry to begin.

An angel, a miracle, or simply God at work?

•   •   •   •   •

It was not our desire to plant just one church. There were over nine hundred towns and villages in the country with no evangelical witness. We desired to plant churches in the main towns and do literature distribution via short visits to smaller towns and some of the larger villages. The two towns we chose for church planting in addition to Bafata were Gabu and Bambadinka. They were the next two largest towns in our target area, and both happened to be on paved roads from Bafata. The entire country had about two hundred total miles of paved roads, so this was a significant consideration. The population of

Bafata was about fifteen thousand people. Gabu may have had four thousand and Bambadinka two thousand. Our goal was to have regular meetings in each of these three towns within our first year.

We had been concentrating our efforts in Bafata. We wanted to make a good start where we lived and establish a valid reputation before expanding our work. We knew that our reputation, good or bad, would precede us—since we were unique in terms of being the only Americans, the only Evangelicals, and almost the only Caucasians in eight thousand square miles. We were a real subject of conversation, so we did our best to encourage the conversation to be positive.

One day two men in a red pickup arrived at our house. The owner of the truck introduced himself. He was Benjamin Constant. He had been born in the Cape Verde Islands but had moved to Guinea-Bissau when he was around twenty years of age. He had met some Nazarene missionaries in Cape Verde who had explained the gospel to him. He then decided to turn from Catholicism and join the Evangelicals. As he had moved to Guinea-Bissau nearly fifty years before meeting us, he had had very little contact with the gospel— maybe two or three times annually when he would visit Bissau. Having heard that we had moved to Bafata as evangelical missionaries, he was there to invite us to come to Gabu to hold meetings in his home.

Our next target was Bambadinka. This is where António and Guiterria lived, already mentioned in chapter four. God had placed them where He knew we would be. We visited many other towns and villages for evangelism. However, it was Gabu and Bambadinka which had been impressed upon our hearts as the targets for our second and third churches. God in His providence had prepared the way for us in each of the two towns. He guided, we merely followed and saw what He had already done.

I mentioned that we often prayed for healing in our churches. It was ordinarily an easy choice, because medical facilities were very limited. And there was often no medicine even in the hospitals.

One time our daughter Becky, during our second or third year in Bafata, developed sores on her head. We anointed her in church but there was no improvement. After praying for her at home, Linda and I felt we should take her to the local hospital. We weren't sure why we should go but we knew it would be interesting. Russia had been sending doctors to Guinea-Bissau to promote the Marxist regime. Under the Portuguese I believe only one citizen of Guinea-Bissau had been trained as a doctor, so most medical workers were foreign "volunteers." Some were from Russia, some from Cuba, some from Red China, and some from Sweden. The doctors at the hospital in Bafata were Russian. We packed a couple of items in a bag and headed to the hospital.

After our initial screening we were shown into a room where a Russian pediatrician and his interpreter met us. The doctor was astounded to see other Caucasians and asked who we were. When he discovered we were Americans he began trying his limited English on us. When we found we could communicate he dismissed the interpreter, closed the door, and began examining Becky's head while we talked. He asked why we were in Guinea-Bissau. We answered we were there to tell the people about God. He began to exclaim in quite a loud voice that this was stupid. There was no God! The Russians sent people like him to give practical help! What we did was useless and wrong! I was impressed by how loudly he spoke, as if someone were listening.

As he continued talking I reached into the bag I was carrying and took out a Russian Bible and a Russian New Testament which I silently showed to him. He whispered, "How much?" and then continued his loud talking. I gave him a price and he purchased the Bible and locked it in his desk. A few moments later he referred us to the dermatologist, also a Russian.

Again we began with the doctor and his interpreter, and again the doctor could speak some English. By the time we left the room the Russian New Testament was safely locked in a desk drawer, and we had some purple medicine for Becky's head. The medicine worked so fast—if it *was* the medicine working—that Becky was well in a couple of days.

Six months later Becky developed similar sores. Again we anointed her with no result. This time we didn't even pray. We just put Russian Scriptures in our bag and headed to the hospital. We found the Russian government had rotated in a new batch of doctors who needed the opportunity to quietly receive God's Word.

This was one reason we did not try to explain when someone we prayed for was not healed right away, or ever. We trusted God to have a reason! In this case we were privileged to learn the reason. It was a different kind of guidance, but the results were certainly divine.

·   ·   ·   ·   ·

This will be my last illustration of guidance. In my dreaming I had made long-range plans about Guinea-Bissau. After four years overseas it was time for us to return to America to visit our families and supporting

churches and friends. Gene and Joan
Cherrington had joined us in Bafata three
months earlier. We turned the work over to
them. After our time in America we would
return and probably move to Gabu. We could
already minister in Portuguese and Crioulo
(pidgin Portuguese, the trade language of
Guinea-Bissau spoken by about thirty percent
of the population). We had made a good start
in Fula, the predominant tribal language of
our area. Becky was already fluent. We would
work from Gabu as we had in Bafata,
beginning another cluster of churches during
our second term, finish learning Fula and start
Mandinka, the language of the other main
Muslim tribe. Then back to America, then a
new location in Guinea-Bissau.

We arrived back in America just before
Thanksgiving, 1979. We had been gone almost
exactly four years. Early in 1980 things
changed.

One day Linda shared with me that she
was not sure she was emotionally able to
return to Guinea-Bissau. What I have not
shared to this point was the tremendous
amount of sickness and hunger and death we
had seen in the country. I already mentioned
that the United Nations had identified it as
the unhealthiest country in the world when
we went there. Some figures we saw indicated
that sixty percent of the children died before

their fifth birthday, and not all of the rest made it to adulthood. While we were there, the country went through a major drought and famine. While we did not see anyone actually starving, most people lacked an adequate diet and were weak. In their weakened condition many became sick and died from the various diseases prevalent in the country. Had it not been for foreign aid from the U.S. and a couple of Western European countries, the losses would have been catastrophic! Linda had paid a high emotional price.

We had to do something. God provided an apartment for us near the shore in New Jersey for several weeks. This was a complex built for missionaries who needed a break. We surely did! Near the end of our time there I felt desperate to hear from God, so I decided to fast and pray for a week. I told Linda that my goal in praying was for her to be enabled to return to the field. She was agreeable to that.

On the fifth day she told me she felt she could go back, but she would like just some small word of confirmation from the Lord. That seemed like the ideal goal for the sixth day of my fast, so I began enthusiastically. Almost as soon as I began to pray I felt the Lord ask me, "What if I tell you to stay?" That seemed like a ridiculous thought, so I tried to bypass it to get to the real business of the day. The

Lord brought me right back to the question. He spent a lot of time that day showing me a lot of my faults: My desire to go back to Guinea-Bissau was motivated by pride, not the love of God. I did not want to be among the statistical fifty percent of missionaries who quit during or immediately after their first term. It was a long and miserable day, but at the end I said to God in all sincerity that if He told us to stay in the States, we would.

I began the seventh day optimistically. God had dealt with Linda and she was ready to go. She would like a bit of confirmation but I knew she would follow wherever He would lead. He had dealt with me. This final day would be the conclusion. Linda would get her assurance. Wrong! As soon as I began to pray I received one word: "Stay!" I relived the sixth day, because what had been hypothetical the day before was now real. I had to go back to the cross. My pride had to be nailed there to die. The final hours of the day were actually good: Once I knew what God wanted, He was gracious to show me some of what He planned to do for us and accomplish through us.

We reported to the mission that we felt God was leading us to stay in the States. At our next annual conference the home staff offered us the Mobilization Department, which has oversight of recruitment and public relations. We have served in that capacity for

19 years. We have had the privilege of participating in the recruiting and training of many excellent missionaries. We live at the headquarters and receive reports of what God is doing around the world.

Do we miss Guinea-Bissau? Yes. Is it hard to be in America instead of on the front line? It is sometimes hard to be in America, but WEC headquarters is *part* of God's front line through the prayer and other ministries that we as a staff, living in community, direct toward many of our fields. The greatest blessing of all is that God has continued to work in us according to His promise of Romans 8:29, conforming us to the image of Jesus.

As I write this book the U.S. staff is creating new positions which they have asked Linda and me to take to increase WEC's capacity as a mission to recruit and train missionaries. In our earlier years our guidance was very personal. Now much of it comes through the WEC staff. We are as confident in group guidance as we are in individual guidance! Our commitment is to follow wherever and however our Lord leads.

Chapter 7

Provision: God's Confirmation of Guidance

In chapter five I wrote about God's provision while I studied at Asbury College and then for one year at Asbury Theological Seminary. By God's grace I began with very little money and graduated with no debt. God called me to prepare for the ministry, He directed me to Asbury, and then He provided what was necessary for me to fulfill His will. In this chapter I want to expand upon this idea, using a number of illustrations to encourage you to believe that God will provide for what He instructs *you* to do.

These illustrations are examples, not models. As examples you will see how God has provided both for me as an individual and for us as a family. In each case we were following the WEC principle of not making our needs known to people—that which C. T. Studd practiced following the example of Hudson Taylor, who followed the example of George Müller.

Let me be clear: This is just one biblical model. There is nothing unscriptural or unspiritual about appeals or solicitations; there is nothing unscriptural or unspiritual about making needs known. The purpose of this chapter is not to establish a formula, but to encourage you to be bold in following God, believing that He will provide everything necessary to fulfill any task or ministry, whether it concerns finances, open doors, wisdom, or anything else.

When Linda and I became engaged, I didn't have money to buy her a ring. However, we did look at rings, dreaming together. We found one she liked and I made the appropriate assurances I would buy this kind when I could. What Linda didn't know was that I almost immediately returned to the store and asked if the ring could be put aside and if I could make payments on it. The owner agreed, and I made a small down payment.

A few weeks later I was part of a witness team of four students sharing about the Asbury revival at a church in Ohio. Almost as soon as the revival began word spread, and students were asked to visit a number of colleges and perhaps hundreds of churches. We basically gave reports and testimonies, and the usual result was that revival spread to whatever church or school the students visited.

At this church we had been given an

offering sufficient to cover the fees for the rental car. I was part of my particular team because none of us had cars and I was the only one old enough to rent one. We never told the churches we had paid to rent a car, but in every case except one they took up an offering that covered our costs and sometimes a bit extra.

There was, as I've indicated, one exception. We were asked to speak at a large church for their Sunday morning service. It was a good service and God moved upon several in the congregation. The pastor thanked us and dismissed us, but with no money and no hint that any was coming. Then, as we were eating at our hosts' home, a call came from a tiny church whose pastor had heard we were there. They asked us to please come and share at their church that day. They set a time and we went. It was a very good service and afterwards they took up a love offering that was probably the largest we ever got!

Getting back to the Ohio meeting . . . we had never seen a service quite like this one. It was customary, after we shared, to give an altar call, inviting anyone who simply wanted to give themselves totally to Christ to come forward. In this service it seemed that nearly half of the congregation came up almost immediately. Everyone else remained in their seats. When we and the pastor had finished praying with those seeking prayer, the pastor was about to dismiss the service when almost *everyone else* got up and came forward without any kind of invitation.

After the service a college student asked to speak to me. He had been away from home and had been saving part of his tithe for some purpose the Lord had not yet shown him. He said he felt he should give the money to *me*. I suggested he give it to the church, but he said God had made it clear that he was to save it and now that he should give it to me! I told him I would take it on one condition: that I would divide it evenly with the rest of the team. He said he didn't care what I did as long as I let him do what he was supposed to do.

I said nothing to the team members right away about the gift because we were so full of joy and praise about the service that we talked about it all during the drive home—about two hours. When we arrived at the school I told about the gift and opened the envelope. The total was five hundred dollars, meaning $125 each. The other three team members had special needs for which this amount was more than adequate. I took my share and went the next morning to the jeweler. I owed exactly one hundred twenty-five dollars.

•   •   •   •   •

Sometimes even when we seem full of faith, God surprises us. After completing the Candidate Orientation Course at the WEC headquarters we asked permission to stay on campus until our first child was born. Linda's prenatal exams had all been at the local hospital, and we hoped to have the baby there. We were given permission to stay. So to use our time well we enrolled at the local Berlitz language school for Portuguese studies. The mission thought this was great.

However, when it was just a day or two before classes were to begin, we didn't have any of the fifteen hundred dollars we needed. We talked to our WEC supervisor and he did something that I don't believe had been done before. He told us that WEC would guarantee payment of our fees. We were to pay something like six hundred dollars for the first block of classes, five hundred for the second, and four hundred for the third.

We arrived at the school with no money, but with a promise from the mission that payment would be made by them within a few days if we personally did not receive the money. The Berlitz director thought this to be absolutely weird, but in order to have our business he agreed. That afternoon we received one hundred fifty dollars from a missionary home on furlough. Within a few days we had the entire six hundred. We took the money to the director and explained how it had come.

When it was time for the second payment he asked if we had the money. It was embarrassing, but we didn't. He accepted the assurance from the mission that we would be covered. Again, all of a sudden we began to receive gifts and within a week we paid. When we began the third and final set of lessons the director told us he wasn't even going to ask if we had the money. He had seen what God had done and was totally confident God would get the money to us. God did and we paid.

The director was a nominal Christian who had never seen God do anything. Through our embarrassment and the subsequent expla- nations, God worked in this man's life and for over a year after our arrival in Africa we corresponded with him and encouraged him.

When Linda and I departed for Portugal for additional language studies in November of 1975, we had sixty dollars per month promised support. That was not nearly enough for any aspect of our necessary support. It would not cover rent, food, or language studies. We did have four hundred dollars in hand, which was enough for our first month.

WEC policy at that time was that when the U.S. staff and the missionary felt it was time to go to the field, the missionary could go as long as he had his air fare. Since the mission did not have a system of pledge cards we did not have a specific amount of support to raise before departure.

Approximately six weeks earlier we had wanted to make final preparations to head to Portugal. We lacked only three things. We had no money to get to Portugal, no place to stay in Portugal, and no support. We had a little cash and that was all. Linda and I had planned that once we had everything we would travel to Ohio to say good-bye to her parents, and then go to North Carolina to say good-bye to my parents. We decided instead to make the good-bye trip first and trust that by the time we finished the trip we would have everything we needed. That's exactly what happened.

The night before we were leaving my parents in North Carolina we received a call from our headquarters. Dr. Bill Livingston, pastor of Bandon Chapel in North Carolina, had just heard about WEC and had called the headquarters to ask if there was someone they could send to his church soon. The following Saturday evening we met with Dr. Livingston, his wife, Sarah, and three couples for a hot dog barbecue. The next morning we shared for ten minutes at the church. The pastor told us he could make no promises of support but he wanted his people to become involved in overseas missions.

Monday we were back in Philadelphia with money for the airline tickets and an address where we could stay in Portugal. We booked the flight and were quickly on our way. At the end of our first month in Portugal we received our next month's remittance, which turned out to be four hundred dollars.

Due to an attempted coup in Portugal and a lot of unrest, we were advised by the leadership of the Guinea-Bissau field to come to Africa as soon as we could, so in January 1966 we flew from Lisbon to Bissau. Interestingly enough, four hundred dollars was still adequate, and that is what we were receiving. Later, when we moved to Bafata and began outreach, our average monthly need rose to six hundred dollars. At that point our average monthly gifts rose to six hundred. The church in North Carolina which had promised nothing began supporting us, and by the time we returned to America they had provided twenty percent of our entire support! God had indeed been faithful.

Chapter 8

Provision:
More Than Money

Money is just one aspect of how God provides. I shared in chapter six how He "provided" the permission for us to move to Bafata through the Marxist government and the Muslim governor. It was one thing to get permission to move to Bafata; it was another thing to find a place to live. During the thirteen-year war many people had fled from Guinea-Bissau to Senegal and the Republic of Guinea. Now that the fighting was over, many were returning and housing was in short supply.

Gene McBride, our field leader, and I decided to drive to Bafata to see if we could get any ideas. We went through all the right channels and were told that accommodations would be very difficult to find. So we just started driving around town, since neither of us had ever seen it. As we passed one house, Gene noticed a lot of sand and gravel piled on the verandah. This was a sign that work was being done on the house. A man was at the front of the building, so we stopped and exchanged greetings. His name was Gibril Balde and he was the owner. In the course of the conversation he explained that he was converting his house (typical mud brick, with a metal roof) from a two-family into a single-family house. He was also putting in a bathroom, because he had heard that white people might be coming to town and he wanted to rent to a white person because they were most likely to pay.

We pointed out the fact that we were white, and said we might be interested in renting the house. We made inquiries about his anticipated asking price, which we did not find satisfactory at that time. Still, we agreed to keep in touch.

A few weeks later Gibril contacted us in Bissau. He had had a financial setback and did not have enough money to finish the remodeling project. He asked if we could lend him the money in exchange for a lower rental price. Gene did the negotiations with him and lent him the money from some available funds the mission had. We set a time to move in, having made arrangements that each month he would receive half the rent and the other half would be counted as a repayment for the loan. We now had a house with an indoor bathroom (no running water, we still had to carry water from the well), rooms for us as a family, and a room with a separate outside entrance we could use as our church. To make the situation even better, our next-door neighbor was one of the most influential Fulas in the area. An angel, a miracle, or simply God at work?

•   •   •   •   •

God supplied another confirmation of our move to Bafata. The move was delayed a couple of months because Gibril could not finish the renovations as quickly as promised. (That was no real surprise.) While we were waiting, a ship from Portugal arrived in Bissau harbor. This may not seem impressive, but at that point very few things were available in stores. It had been weeks since we were able to buy soap, matches, or even oil for our lantern, toothpaste, toilet paper, batteries and many such "necessities." This ship was *loaded* with household goods! We bought a good stock of non-perishable items as well as some basic food supplies.

The story gets better. Just before the ship arrived we had received our monthly remittance from America. This time we received fifteen hundred dollars! Most of it was from a special offering taken by Dr. Livingston and the people at Bandon Chapel. In order for the money to be in our hands when needed, it had been given two months earlier. From Bandon Chapel it was sent to the WEC office in Pennsylvania. It remained there until the proper day of the month when all the accumulated money for all our missionaries in Guinea-Bissau was put together and sent to us by air mail. It arrived in Guinea-Bissau two to three weeks later. Then it had to go into the local banking system to be converted into the local currency. Only then could we get it and spend it. Dr. Livingston and the people at the church had no idea that they were part of God's perfect timing when they sent the gift.

We also rented a truck for the move to Bafata. Once we moved into the house I made a comment to Linda that God had blessed so much that we did not need much money the next month, only a little for fresh food. The next month our total support was ninety-two dollars, and the mission added one hundred more because they were concerned. We didn't need the extra hundred. God's timing and provision had been perfect.

We were able to buy a small bottled-gas cooking stove. Naturally, we had to buy some bottles of gas. These were extremely hard to get, but we got two from the seller of the stove and two from someone else. After several months we knew that if we were very frugal, a bottle might last thirty-two days; if we did nothing special to conserve gas, the bottle would last twenty-seven or twenty-eight days. Therefore we would normally use up three bottles, put on the fourth, and then make the two-hundred-mile round trip to Bissau to trade in the three empty bottles for three full ones. Bissau was the only place to get full bottles.

Our third year in Guinea-Bissau we were approaching the Christmas season. We were scheduled to go to Bissau in six weeks. God had provided some flour and sugar, so Linda was going to do some Christmas baking. The second bottle ran out and I connected the third. As I opened the valve, gas began escaping into the kitchen. I immediately closed the valve and, upon close inspection, I found a tiny hole in the bottle. It was in such a place that if we opened the valve at all, the gas leaked. I tried two or three household patches, but none held. So I removed the bottle and put on the last one. Now we had a problem. Not only were Linda and Becky and I living in the house, but so was Rute, the daughter of a man with leprosy. We had an arrangement that she could live with us and go to school in exchange for housework for Linda. We also were boarding Joaquim, a school teacher and one of the finest Christians in the country. He had been transferred to Bafata to teach in the high school.

We calculated that if we abandoned the idea of any Christmas baking, cooked one less meal per day, and made Joaquim and Rute either eat with us or eat cold food, we would still run out of gas ten or twelve days before our scheduled trip. (Joaquim taught in the evening and generally ate supper afterwards, about three hours after we had eaten. Rute often waited to eat with him.) If we ran out of gas we would have to get wood or charcoal and cook outside. After thinking and praying, we decided to cook as if we had all the gas in the world. Linda would bake Christmas cookies and cakes, Joaquim and Rute would have warm meals, and when the gas ended we would get charcoal and cook on the ground like most of our neighbors did on a regular basis.

After twenty-five days we knew the bottle had to be empty, but every time we lit the stove there was still a little more. Forty-one days after I attached the bottle, we ran out of gas. It was the night before we were to leave for Bissau the next morning. An angel, a miracle, or simply God at work?

•   •   •   •   •

We have other stories that show how God used special provision to confirm that we were indeed doing what He wanted, but let's jump forward to around 1984. We were then on home staff back in America. The staff as a group felt we needed another residential building on campus because of the increasing number on home staff and the increasing numbers of people training to go overseas, as well as a few retirees from the field living with us. God provided a group of workers from HIM (Helps International Ministries) who agreed to provide labor for free as long as we provided room, board, and materials. The mission had a little over $10,000 with which to begin the project that would cost over $700,000. We were committed to the WEC policy of not making our needs known. We began. Time and time again God provided either money or material.

One day we came to a crisis point. We had used all available money and we needed a large amount for essential supplies. We estimated we needed nearly $100,000 immediately, and we had nothing. We gathered for a day of prayer to ask God to send funds. When the morning mail arrived there was an envelope with a letter and a set of keys.

Ed and Wyn Hancox had served WEC for many years in Africa and then in North Carolina as recruiters. They had retired and were living in a house in North Carolina owned by the mission. On very short notice someone in North Carolina provided for them to move into a retirement facility. They didn't call the headquarters but just moved, and sent the keys to us. The next day, Peter Ellis and I got into his car to drive to North Carolina to check on the house and see if we could begin the process of selling it. We arrived in Charlotte the next morning and visited a Christian realtor who supported some WEC missionaries. He agreed to be the agent for the sale. He sent someone to put up a For Sale sign, and as he was hammering the sign into the ground someone driving by saw him, asked about the house, and agreed to our price. We came back to WEC with about $94,000. We never had to stop construction of the building due to lack of funds!

These have been some of the unusual accounts. Most of the time nothing so spectacular happens. Linda and I joined WEC in 1974, and from that time have never had a promised salary. God has consistently met all our needs and those of our other WEC personnel.

Chapter **9**

Car Problems

I am not a mechanic. I have learned to do a lot of little things on cars over the years, but I cannot do anything major. God has been gracious to me in my ignorance. He has also used some car problems in order to encourage me and bring glory to Himself.

When Linda and I were WEC candidates, we took a short trip to New Jersey to visit one of my father's brothers. As Snoopy would say, "It was a dark and stormy night." Just as we arrived at my uncle's home the water pump blew. We had almost no money and certainly no ability to do anything. However, my aunt's son (second marriage) was there and he liked messing with cars. He was able to get a water pump for us and install it while the car was sitting in the driveway. We had enough money to pay for the pump, and the next day we drove back to WEC. It was a little thing, but a big encouragement to us.

A couple of years later we were in Guinea-Bissau. Someone had sent a gift to the mission specifically to provide a vehicle for someone in "a pioneer evangelism ministry" who seemed to need a car but had no way to buy one. We knew nothing about this until we received word from the States that this gift had come and we had been chosen! We were able to get a new Volkswagen van. It was ideal. When we went to Gabu or Bambadinka or Contubuel (the site of our fourth congregation) we could take a group of believers from Bafata with us. They encouraged the other groups and received additional teaching by being with us.

Gasoline was fairly difficult to get. Most of the time I had to buy a fifty-five gallon drum of gas and store it in the garage we had built onto the house. I would siphon gas from the drum into a five gallon plastic container, filtering it as I did so in order to remove impurities, and then pour the gas into the tank of the car. After a while it was impossible to get gasoline anywhere except in Bissau. I was later able to get a second drum. When we would make our rare trips to Bissau, I would take the empty drum to the gasoline storage area and trade it for a full one—of course, paying for the gas, which cost over two dollars per gallon.

One day when we were in Bissau I saw a line at one of the traditional gas stations. A supply of gasoline had arrived from Portugal, so the stations had been allowed to fill their tanks and sell to customers. I delightedly got in line and got the VW tank filled. Less than half a mile later I saw a lot of cars stopped. Suddenly our car stopped too. The managers of the gas station had wanted to make the gas last longer, so they had added water to it. They added too much, as a number of frustrated drivers could verify. I walked to our headquarters and Hans Frinzel, a Dutch WECer, came back to the car with me. Hans was not a mechanic but he was good with cars. We siphoned the gas from the tank into a couple of plastic containers. Then Hans took apart the carburetor right there and cleaned the water out of it. He made me do it too. Then we poured gas from another container into the car and back to the mission we went. Later Hans poured the watery gas through a chamois cloth and salvaged it for later use. Again, it was not dramatic, but it was a blessing to us.

A couple of years later, after our return to America, Linda and I were given a Chevrolet Malibu station wagon by my parents. It had two hundred twenty thousand miles on it, but it ran well and had never had a major problem. We drove it for another fifty thousand miles.

One weekend we were asked to speak at a church in Pittsburgh, Pennsylvania, about 280 miles from WEC. As we drove through the mountains on the Pennsylvania Turnpike, we had a problem. The car really struggled up hills, although it did great on the way down. Our fuel pump was dying. We made it to Pittsburgh, but as we drove through the city we had lots of problems. It was too late to do anything that night.

The next day our host offered to help me find a garage that could work on the car. I was ready to agree, but felt a strong check from the Lord that I should not do it. I thanked our host but said I felt we just should not do it on Sunday. That afternoon we prepared to head back through the mountains to Philadelphia. Our host family thought we were a bit crazy and probably overly legalistic. I basically felt the same, except I had a very strong conviction not to get the car worked on that day *and* not to wait until Monday to return home. We did pray over the car, and Linda and Becky and I started back. We had absolutely no problem. We arrived back at WEC after a pleasant and uneventful drive. The next morning I wondered what to do. Had God "healed" the fuel pump? I took the car for a drive and within half a mile realized the healing was very temporary. So I bought a new fuel pump and installed it, and that solved the problem until we sold the car.

Is it wrong to repair a car on Sunday? It was for us that Sunday. God used that event to show us that He might occasionally ask something that seemed strange, but if we obeyed He would take care of us and it would be a testimony to someone.

One more car story is enough. Linda's father taught auto mechanics. He was a bit concerned about the old cars we got, so he decided to bless us. He had a used car that he wanted to trade to me because he knew it was better than what we had. He fixed everything that he imagined could cause us a problem.

Even a top mechanic can't keep God from stopping a car for His glory. I was on my way home from representing WEC at Houghton College in upstate New York. About a half hour from Houghton a radiator hose blew and I had to stop. There was a house nearby. I knocked on the door to ask about using the phone. No one was home. So I sat by the car until someone stopped and volunteered to take me to the nearby town of Angelica to see if I could get a hose from the Western Auto store.

The manager of the store said they didn't have the proper hose, but his son would be coming home from work in a couple of hours and he would have him pick up a hose on the way and bring it to me out at my car.

As I talked to the manager I noticed he had some literature about abortion. I asked about it and he explained he was part of a local pro-life organization. We talked a while longer and I discovered he was Roman Catholic, and although very religious and active in the church, he seemed to have no understanding of what it meant to be born again. He felt he was saved by infant baptism and maintained his standing with God through the church. I shared the gospel with him the best I could, but he was not ready to make a change.

Later his son brought me the hose. I fixed the car, added what spare water I had—which was enough to get me to the next town where I got more water—and continued home.

About twelve years later I was speaking at Elohim Bible Institute in the same area of New York. One of the teachers decided to talk with me afterward. I asked where he was from, and he laughingly said, "Someplace you certainly don't know—Angelica, New York." I told him I knew Angelica and related the story of the burst hose. He beamed and told me that the manager of the Western Auto store had died about two years earlier, but a month before he died he had led him to salvation in Jesus. Had God wanted me to be a part in a parade of witnesses to this man? I don't know for sure, but it seems God allowed me to hear the rest of the story for some reason.

I have no idea which is the greater blessing. Was it the cousin who replaced a water pump in his backyard in New Jersey?

Was it having Hans available to clean the carburetor in Bissau? Was it having God apparently heal a fuel pump for the Sunday drive from Pittsburgh to Philadelphia? Was it having a radiator hose burst alongside a highway in New York? Each of the four was an encouragement to my faith.

Chapter 10

Protection

In this chapter I want to give a few examples of what may be some of the more dramatic episodes we have experienced in our service for Jesus.

There is a big difference between presumption and faith. Presumption is a form of foolishness in which someone feels he doesn't have to take precautions or obey laws, because God will take care of him. When I was pastoring in Ohio a local man visited the evening service. When it came time for testimonies, he shared how he had been driving down the highway when God impressed him to pray. He was a little fearful, but he obeyed God, shut his eyes, and began to pray—while still driving. He used this as an illustration of faith and protection. Most of us thought it would have been a good idea to pull off the highway, stop, and then pray. Happily, he had not had a wreck. However, while you can't prove such a person to be wrong, this apparently presumptuous confidence is not what I would call the normal model of faith.

Faith is obeying God, even if what He is calling you to do seems impossible. While obeying, you take appropriate precautions. You get vaccinations before going overseas. You take prophylactic medications in malarial zones. You lock your house at night and you lock your car. You don't walk around with a roll of cash in your hand.

When does one cross the line between faith and presumption? Only God knows. When Linda and I went to Guinea-Bissau with Becky we felt we were obeying God in faith. My father felt we were being presumptuous by taking our daughter to the unhealthiest country in the world. In his mind, just because she (and we) survived, it did not prove we were right.

There does seem to be a very thin line between faith and presumption. Gideon attacked the Midianites with three hundred men. Moses took the Israelites to the Red Sea—which left them no way of escape when Pharaoh's troops approached. Shadrach, Meshach, and Abednego told King Nebuchadnezzar that God would deliver them from the furnace, and then added these words, "but if not . . ."

Faith is quite often going into a situation somewhat blindly. It is trusting God for safety and for deliverance. Two people describing the actions of some of our missionaries may view the same event differently. One will be amazed at their faith. The other will cringe at their presumption.

As you read these accounts, I hope you will not think I acted with a presumptuous attitude. I really did not do anything to put myself or my family into the particular situations, unless you count driving to be presumptuous. We did sometimes find ourselves in danger, and God did deliver us. An angel, a miracle, or simply God at work? It's your call.

·   ·   ·   ·   ·

Earlier I shared that one of the considerations for beginning work in Gabu and Bambadinka was because they were on paved roads that connected them with Bafata. Please don't use American highways as a comparison. These paved roads were about sixteen feet wide, barely wide enough for two trucks to pass each other carefully. The grass was not cut back by any state highway department. Instead, during the rainy season it began to grow right at the edge of the highway. By the time the dry season arrived the grass was commonly eight to ten feet high and sometimes arched over the road like a canopy. Eventually the local people would cut the grass and carry it away in bundles to replace the grass roofs of their houses. Then fires would be started that would burn most of the remnant. This was done on purpose to avoid wildfires that could destroy entire villages.

For several months of the six-month rainy season and the first couple of months of the dry, we would have no idea when someone or something might step out of the high grass onto the highway. There were less than ten thousand vehicles in the entire country. Most of them were in or near the capital. So people often walked along the highway because it was open and smooth. Hopefully they would listen for a vehicle before stepping out from the grass, but often they seemed preoccupied. The cattle and other livestock simply didn't care about traffic at all.

One Tuesday night we were making the 32-mile trip from Gabu to Bafata. The VW van was full of believers from Bafata. The road was basically straight, with one curve near Gabu and two near Bafata. Otherwise it was like an arrow. We were going along at about fifty miles an hour, with the lights on high, when all of a sudden I hit the brakes and swerved. Only one other person saw the black bull that had just come from the grass onto the highway—into our lane!

Another night we were returning from

Gabu when we saw a vehicle coming the other way. We slowed down to about thirty-five because it was difficult to see, due to their lights. The instant the other car passed the only thing I could see was the truck that was stopped in our lane—with no lights or reflectors! I jerked the wheel as hard as I could and almost scraped the truck. There was no one around the truck and it had not been on the road when we went to Gabu. There was absolutely no kind of reflector on the back! We swallowed our hearts and continued. Somehow we didn't think *God* was the one who caused the truck to break down and be parked, or who caused the other car to come with its lights practically blinding us at the exact time we approached the truck. We did know for certain that God allowed *me* to see it and *swerve*, missing the truck without flipping the van. Interestingly enough, the exact same scenario took place about two months later. After that, I came to a near stop whenever cars approached us on the Gabu-Bafata road at night.

I told in the previous chapter how we bought contaminated gas in Bissau, but due to God's goodness and Hans' mechanical knowledge we cleaned the carburetor and replaced the gas. However, there was apparently still some water in the tank, plus a few other items. The van began stalling as we were driving. If I would let it sit, we could start again and go for a while. Maybe we would have no more problems for a day or two, or maybe we were good for five miles. No fun.

One day I decided to test my mechanical ignorance and inability. I put a bamboo mat on the dirt floor of our garage, took a flashlight and crawled under the van. Since I'm not totally ignorant, I recognized the fuel tank and found the fuel line coming from the tank to the engine. There was a clear plastic filter on the line. The filter was absolutely clogged with rust and gunk. Since replacement filters were not available I decided to drain the gas tank, remove the filter, reinstall it, and see what happened. It actually worked well, for a couple of days. Then it was clogged again. I decided on a more radical approach. I had a piece of narrow plastic hose that was designed to be part of the air filtering system for an aquarium. My plan was now to disconnect the fuel line, attach this hose, and drain gasoline from the tank. When the flow would slow to a trickle, I would remove the small hose and run a small piece of wire through the short outlet pipe into the tank to attempt to break loose the blockage.

The procedure was working well, although I was getting quite wet. Every time the flow stopped and I disconnected the aquarium hose, any gas in the hose came down my arm onto my shirt or onto the bamboo mat. I kept at it for quite a while, even pouring gasoline back into the tank because I was getting a lot of rust and residue. After an hour or so, my skin was burning and my head was spinning.

Then I learned something about working on cars. Always disconnect the battery. Very close to the gas tank outlet was the solenoid, part of the electrical system. While my reaming wire was in the gas tank I accidentally touched the solenoid with the other end. The wire basically vaporized and I was lying on my back looking at a stream of fire shooting from the outlet right over my face. I was amazingly peaceful as I thought, "So this is how I'll die." However, after a second or so I realized I *hadn't* ignited and the air which was actually full of gasoline vapors had *not* exploded. I remembered the drum of gasoline stored in the garage just in front of the car, and the fact that Linda and Becky were inside the house. What would happen to *them* if the *drum* exploded?

I have no idea how long it took for those thoughts to go through my muddled mind. I realized that maybe I could do something, so I raised my head and blew out the flame. End of story! An angel, a miracle, or simply God at work?

A few months later the teenage son of

one of the evangelists in Bissau died. He had been doing some painting and had gotten about one quarter of a cup of gasoline to use to wash the paint from his hands and arms. He was walking with the open container of gas and passed about ten feet from an open fire. The gas in the can exploded and the boy was burned so severely that he died within a couple of days. I had had much more gasoline all over me and I was within an inch of the flame! God's ways are indeed mysterious.

• • • • •

I've already mentioned that I wonder if even *driving* is presumptuous. A number of my interesting experiences have occurred very near home in Philadelphia.

One morning I was about a mile from home on a four-lane highway divided by a metal railing. A large truck was approaching from the other direction when I saw an entire wheel come off the rear of the cab. It actually passed the cab, nearly causing a wreck as the driver stared at it rolling by. The wheel hit a bump, jumped the median, and came right at me. Fortunately I had about fifty yards to plan my strategy and I was the only car in the immediate area. I simply stopped, and the wheel began to wobble and flopped in front of me.

One day a few months later I was on Interstate 76 in downtown Philadelphia. I was behind a truck carrying a load of plywood sheets. Something snapped and suddenly sheets of plywood came flying off the truck. The first one barely missed me. By then I and everyone behind me began stopping. Nobody hit me from behind and nothing hit from in front or above.

Another time I left the WEC campus and was merging onto the four-lane highway that connects a few hundred yards away. As I merged into the empty right lane a large truck with a load of barrels passed in the left lane. The tailgate of the truck swung open and it began raining barrels, which bounced and rolled all over the highway. They hit all around my car, but not one even touched me.

I have had more of the same kinds of experiences, but I hope you see that it is *God* who is our safety and our deliverance. He is perfectly capable of taking care of us in any situation. Obedience to Him puts us in His hand, the safest place I know.

Now one last story for this chapter. The WEC campus has a long driveway that connects it to the public street in front of the property. That street then merges into the highway I have mentioned twice in this chapter. Our children would walk to the bottom of the driveway and wait for the school bus to stop so they could board. For the first year or so the bus stopped on the other side of the road and the children would cross the street. Since some of the children were young and since several families were involved, we always had at least one adult go down with the children.

One morning the bus stopped and the children began to cross the street, not following one another in a file but in one broad line. The parent standing behind them said that suddenly it was as if they hit an invisible waist-high barrier that abruptly stopped them. At that moment a car that had not stopped for the bus passed within a couple of feet of our line of children. After that the bus driver changed his route so that he stopped on *our* side of the street, so the children didn't have to cross to the bus anymore.

Was this apparent act of protection for our children an angel, a miracle, or simply an act of God?

Chapter 11

The Fruit of Simply Doing

We were told the work among the Islamic Fula and Mandinka tribes would be difficult. Wouldn't we prefer to work among one of the animistic tribes that was already responsive to the gospel? Were we ready for years of hard work with little fruit? Even the members of the nearly fifty churches in the western half of Guinea-Bissau believed Muslims would *not* come to Christ. When we moved to Bafata, therefore, we had fairly realistic expectations of what we would probably face. But in some ways we were overly pessimistic. Why? Probably, because we had forgotten one factor—that WEC had been praying for nearly twenty years for someone to work with these Muslim tribes. Twenty years of accumulated prayer is a very powerful force. God did grant fruit, though not in the manner we expected; and looking back from now to our four years there, we may have a glimpse of His strategy—which is far better than ours.

We did find the Muslims resistant, although not antagonistic on the whole. In fact, in the four churches we planted only about five of the total converts were former Muslims. The majority were from several animistic tribes. And Benjamin Constant of Gabu was from a Catholic background. But we went to win Muslims! Did we fail? We can have our opinions. God is the one who has the answer. Let me give a few vignettes.

Reputation is essential in ministry. God used a number of the converts from the non-Muslim tribes to establish a positive reputation for the gospel. A lot of this may have been because of the clear message we proclaimed. Peter says that we are "partakers of the divine nature" (2 Peter 1:4). We preached this as being the normative result of receiving Jesus as Savior and Lord. Conversion was not merely mental assent that Jesus is the Son of God, but a full life transformation. When Paul told the Philippian jailer (Acts 16:31) that he had to "believe on the Lord Jesus Christ" in order to be saved, he was telling this man who was a loyal Roman that he had to profess that Jesus, who is the Christ, was his Lord. In other words, he had to reject Caesar who also claimed to be Lord. And he did so with great joy.

When someone told me he wanted to become a believer in Christ, I would usually reply, "No, you can't." Naturally, this puzzled the person, so of course he asked why. I would explain that because he had seen God doing good things in the lives of other people it was quite likely he wanted the same workings in his own life—but he really had no idea what Jesus required of him. I would then offer to teach the inquirer the Word of God for about two weeks (many hours) and after that time let him make a decision. During that time I clearly explained that he could not add the name of Jesus to the other names he already invoked (which was what some wanted). Also, Jesus was not promising perfect health, many children, or any of the other dreams many had. Instead, Jesus offered to drive Satan from the believer's heart, forgive his sins, and then come and live in him through His Spirit and so give him a new life. But, I stressed, the individual had to now belong to Jesus as fully as he had belonged to the animistic spirits he formerly feared and served. I explained that this would mean alienation from one's family, probable persecution, and maybe even death. (And we call the gospel "good news"?)

Let me digress to say that we generally did not use the word "Christian" to describe ourselves. For five hundred years "Christian" meant Catholic, so we were "believers," "Evangelicals," or "Protestants," but we rarely used or were given the title "Christian." It had very negative connotations.

A few days into the teaching process I would ordinarily be asked a number of questions that would go something like this: "The Bible says the Spirit of God will come and live in my heart?" Yes. "You say this is the Spirit of the God who created the universe and raised Jesus from the dead?" Yes. "If I become a believer in Jesus, the Spirit of God will not share my heart with the tribal spirits? He will make them leave because He wants my whole heart?" Yes. "The Spirit of God is strong enough to do this and the evil spirits will never be able to drive the Spirit of God away?" Yes. "I will be free from the control of the spirits that have been in me?" Yes.

At that point inquirers understood the power of God and were eager to receive Jesus and the freedom He brought. They understood they were agreeing to be slaves to God, because they had been slaves to the satanic spirits. They knew the misery the evil spirits brought and they knew the good the Spirit of God would bring. They were eager to be filled with the Spirit of God so there would be no room for Satan.

As a result of this high level of pre-conversion teaching, the change in the lives of those who came to Christ was generally dramatic, a true change from night to day, from darkness to light, from evil to good.

Within a year an astounding teaching was being voiced in the main mosque in Bafata, the main mosque in our half of the country: "Pagans go to hell because they don't know about God. Catholics go to hell because they worship idols. Muslims go to heaven because they are Muslims. Evangelicals have wrong doctrine—but their lives are so superior to ours, they must go to heaven!" Muslims had very high moral teachings, but they confessed they had no power to attain the standards of their own teaching. Our believers were living what Muslims desired! Therefore in the eyes of many we were "good." Muslims were zealous to win pagans to Islam, but it began to be taught that if a pagan would not become a Muslim, he should be advised to become an Evangelical.

This did not mean we were accepted by everyone. There were radical Muslims who wanted us kicked out of the country. There were some from Muslim and/or pagan backgrounds who had curses put on us, or at least on me. However, on the whole we were seen as "good" by most of the people of Bafata, and therefore by those to whom they talked.

Perhaps the most dramatic transformation came in the life of Benjamin Constant, whom I mentioned in chapter six. Constant, as he preferred to be called, declared himself to be an Evangelical although he knew almost

nothing of the gospel. He simply knew that
about fifty years earlier he had quit being a
Catholic in order to become an Evangelical.
When he moved to Guinea-Bissau from the
Cape Verde Islands he developed a business
that made him one of the wealthiest men in
the country. He bought honey from those who
"harvested" it from trees throughout the
country and sold it to a distillery which made
extremely potent alcohol. He saw no problem
with alcohol production or consumption. He
himself drank a considerable amount daily.

During the weekly meetings at his home
I did not mention the things most Christians
do and the things from which they usually
abstain. I did not want to develop a group of
people who showed outward conformity with
no true inward change. Rather, we taught from
the Bible, and emphasized again and again
the freedom and power and holiness and joy
that are products of participating in the divine
nature, of being totally given to Jesus.

One day Constant and his driver came to
Bafata and asked me to accompany them on a
short trip because Constant wanted to talk.
(Constant was a large man, as was his driver.
I was squeezed between them in the cab of
the small pickup while we traveled.) Constant
was as excited as a young child on Christmas
morning. He began by telling me how much
He loved God. He talked of having faith like

a little child. He was excited and bubbly, and of course I wondered where the conversation was going. I found out. Constant said, "Jesus turned water into wine." I agreed. He said, "Jesus drank wine." Again I agreed. Then he said, "If Jesus was in Guinea-Bissau, He wouldn't drink!" I was curious and asked why. He then told me of all the evils in the lives of men and women who were addicted to alcohol. It was the finest temperance lecture I have ever heard. Constant concluded by announcing that having realized this, he had quit drinking alcohol—cold turkey. Alcohol was an evil that was controlling him, and it was inconsistent with his claim that the Spirit of God controlled him, so he quit!

The effect was so dramatic that I had a merchant friend of Constant's in Bafata ask me what had happened. But that was only the beginning. A few weeks later, Constant invited me for another ride. He said God's Spirit had shown him that anything to do with the production or sale of alcohol was wrong for him, so he had taken most of his money and had given it to all those who had become his dependents because of his wealth! He told them to be careful because he was quitting his business and would not be getting money to give to them. (His income dropped from the equivalent of a millionaire to very little immediately.)

He died a few months later, probably from cirrhosis of the liver brought on by fifty years of drinking. Hundreds of the leading citizens of Guinea-Bissau came to his funeral and heard the gospel message that had transformed Constant.

Because of the committed group of believers in Bafata, the positive reputation of the gospel was established there.

Because of Constant the gospel was seen as positive in Gabu.

Because of António, Guiterria, Adolfo and Quinta, it was seen as positive in Bambadinka.

From these three central towns the news spread to many smaller towns and villages. In other words, God used former pagans and a former Catholic to show the power of God to Muslims.

I haven't mentioned the fourth congregation, in Contubuel. This happened almost accidentally. The government planned an agricultural project in Contubuel, about fifteen miles from us in a different direction from either Gabu or Bambadinka. They imported their laborers from near Bissau. One of these men was a Christian who knew about us. He lived in Bafata to be near our church and caught a ride on a government truck to Contubuel for work. He was witnessing, and some of his fellow workers were coming to Christ, so I started going there regularly to teach. However, when the short project was over, the entire group was transferred elsewhere, so it did not become a permanent church.

•   •   •   •   •

What has happened in the twenty years since we left? Other missionaries and national workers carried on the work in Bafata. The church is well established and embraces believers from a number of tribes, including former Muslims.

Youth With A Mission (YWAM) got permission to come into Gabu with a medical project. They later started a Christian elementary school. They took our small group of believers and the reputation of the gospel and have built a strong work with dozens of Muslim converts. Adolfo of Bambadinka was transferred to Bissau for a while, and then he went to Bible school. He went back to Bambadinka as a pastor/evangelist and saw many saved. The Bible school for the entire Evangelical Church of Guinea-Bissau was moved close to him and Quinta. Now they have moved to another nearby town to start over, and already they have a thriving church. Adolfo also spent over a year in England to learn English so he could read books about how to win Muslims to Jesus. I think English is his sixth language.

Eusébio, first mentioned in chapter four, also went to Bible school. He is now pastoring a church of hundreds in Bissau and trains church-planting teams. He too was able to go to England to learn English to be better equipped to win Muslims. Another man, José Manuel, who is one of the many I haven't mentioned in the book, also completed Bible Institute with his wife and they are serving the Lord and His church.

When Linda and I went to Bafata it was with a vision to reach Muslims. National Christians were not "wasting their time" with such "foolishness." However, God has worked so that there are still missionaries working among Muslims, but He has now given vision to the national church, which has to be involved and must welcome former Muslims if the body of Christ is to be whole. This is simply God at work.

Conclusion

Does it take a miracle to make our faith sure? As I said in the Introduction, I am not sure I have ever seen a miracle. *I have seen God do many wonderful things!* Perhaps the greatest of these is the absolute transformation of men and women who were dedicated to satanic spirits and were brought up under the teaching and control of these spirits all their lives—until they came to know Jesus!

I have one more story. In early 1976, after Linda and I had been in Guinea-Bissau just a couple of months, a sickness simply called "the fever" struck. It seemed to affect only children, and it appeared to have a one hundred percent mortality rate. Many children died in the hospital and many others died at home.

One day our daughter, Becky, came down with the fever. She was less than a year old. Linda and I watched her lying on her bed, not eating or drinking, not crying or making any significant movement. We had already been advised to let her die at home rather than take her to the hospital where she would unquestionably die—one of many in a shared bed.

I asked Linda, "What will you do if Becky dies?" She replied, "I'll cry, but I'll never turn my back on God's calling." As the hours passed, I suddenly remembered what James had written, that any who were sick should call the elders and be prayed for and anointed. Becky, of course, was too young to ask for such help. As her father, I went immediately and asked one of our other missionaries and one of the national pastors who lived nearby to anoint and pray for her. They did, and that same day she got up from her bed. The next, she was playing as if she had never been sick.

Had we seen a miracle in the healing of our daughter? We think so, but how can we verify such a thing? The point I want to make is that Linda's faith was already *established* because *she knew her heavenly Father*. She did not need a miracle to know who He is and what He could do! Seeing our daughter get well encouraged us—however, it encouraged the faith we *already had*.

I have recounted dozens of remarkable events in this book. They are part of our lives, part of our history. They have helped make us who we are now; but I honestly don't think our faith is any greater now than it was in

1968, or 1976, or any other year. We are definitely more experienced and, we trust, more knowledgeable. Perhaps we are also better at keeping our eyes on Jesus on a daily basis.

We are simply determined to *follow Jesus*. And we encourage you to do the same. Look back in your life. Record the things you know God has done in your life. Were these evidence of angels, miracles, or simply God at work? Does it really matter? *God* did them. Keep these in your memory and put your focus on *Jesus*, the Author and Perfecter of your faith. Follow the Good Shepherd.